I Can Be Anything!

I CAN BE A BASEBALL PLAYER

By Nancy Greenwood

Please visit our website, www.garethstevens.com. For a free color catalog of all our high-quality books, call toll free 1-800-542-2595 or fax 1-877-542-2596.

Library of Congress Cataloging-in-Publication Data
Names: Greenwood, Nancy, author. | Gareth Stevens Publishing.
Title: I can be a baseball player / Nancy Greenwood.
Other titles: I can be anything!
Description: New York : Gareth Stevens Publishing, 2021. | Series: I can be anything! | Includes index. | Contents: Hello, Mr. Smith! – Around the bases – Getting started – Let's be baseball players! – Words to know – Index.
Identifiers: LCCN 2019044945 | ISBN 9781538255605 (Library Binding) | ISBN 9781538255582 (Paperback) | ISBN 9781538255612 (eBook) | ISBN 9781538255599 (6 Pack)
Subjects: LCSH: Baseball players–Juvenile literature. | Baseball–Juvenile literature. | Baseball for children–Juvenile literature. | Major League Baseball (Organization) | Readers.
Classification: LCC GV867.5 .G755 2020 | DDC 796.357–dc23
LC record available at https://lccn.loc.gov/2019044945

First Edition

Published in 2021 by
Gareth Stevens Publishing
111 East 14th Street, Suite 349
New York, NY 10003

Editor: Kate Mikoley
Designer: Laura Bowen

Photo credits: Cover, p. 1 (kid) RichVintage/E+/Getty Images; cover, p.1 (background) JHENG YAO/Shutterstock.com; pp. 5, 7, 24 (pitcher) sirtravelalot/Shutterstock.com; p. 9 zsolt_uveges/Shutterstock.com; pp. 11, 17 Jan de Wild/Shutterstock.com; pp. 13, 24 (base) ecliptic blue/Shutterstock.com; p. 15 antpkr/Shutterstock.com; p. 19 Aspen Photo/Shutterstock.com; p. 21 TerryJ/iStock/Getty Images Plus/Getty Images; p. 23 Ariel Skelley/DigitalVision/Getty Images.

Printed in the United States of America

Some of the images in this book illustrate individuals who are models. The depictions do not imply actual situations or events.

CPSIA compliance information: Batch #CS20GS: For further information contact Gareth Stevens, New York, New York at 1-800-542-2595.

Contents

Mr. Smith plays baseball.
It's his job!

He's a pitcher.
A pitcher throws
the ball.

A batter tries to hit it.
They use a bat.

A hit means you run!

A baseball field has four bases.

They are first,
second, and third.
The last is home plate.

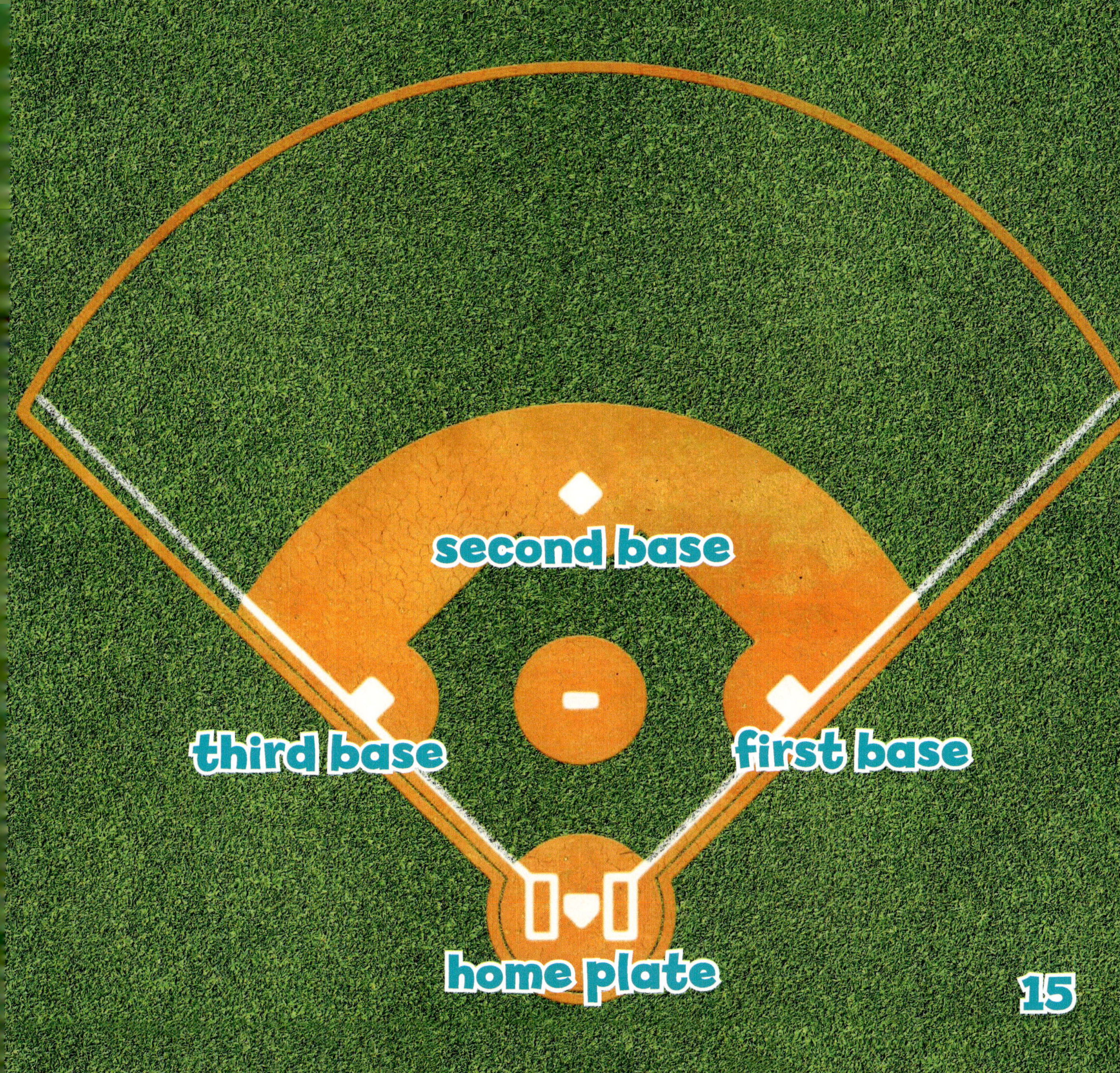
second base
third base
first base
home plate

Running to all bases is called a run.

A home run is running
to all bases in a row!

I play T-ball.
Mr. Smith did too!

I can be a
baseball player.
So can you!

Words to Know

base

pitcher

Index